SELLING OURSELVES

MARKETING BODY IMAGES

by Barb Palser

Content Consultant: John V. Pavlik,
Professor and Chair, Department of Journalism and Media Studies,
School of Communication and Information, Rutgers University

COMPASS POINT BOOKS
a capstone imprint

EXPLORING
MEDIA LITERACY

Compass Point Books
1710 Roe Crest Drive
North Mankato, MN 56003

Editors: Mari Kesselring and Lauren Coss
Designers: Becky Daum and Christa Schneider

Image Credits:
Alexander Zhiltsov/iStockphoto, cover; Marion Curtis/AP Images, back cover (left);
Cameron Whitman/iStockphoto, back cover (center); Niko Guido/iStockphoto, back
cover (right); Monkey Business Images/Shutterstock Images, 5, 55 (top); Richard
Levine/Alamy, 6; Red Line Editorial, 8, 26, 28, 62; Thaksina Khaikaew/AP Images,
11; Hassan Ammar/AP Images, 13; Yuri Arcurs/Shutterstock Images, 15, 42; Jaren
Wicklund/iStockphoto, 16; Shea Walsh/AP Images, 19; Paul Drinkwater/AP Images,
20; Blackwater Images/iStockphoto, 21; Huntstock.com/Shutterstock Images, 23;
Zhu Difeng/Shutterstock Images, 25; Stefano Lunardi/Shutterstock Images, 29;
Eleanor Bentall/Bloomberg/Getty Images, 30; Jeff Chiu/AP Images, 32; Pash/OK/
Shutterstock Images, 33; iStockphoto, 35, 37, 45, 46, 65; Lev Radin/Shutterstock
Images, 36; Gene Chutka/iStockphoto, 39; Trae Patton/NBC/NBCU Photo Bank/AP
Images, 48; Stuart Ramson/AP Images, 51; John M. Heller/Getty Images, 52; Charles
Sykes/AP Images, 53; Buena Vista Pictures/Photofest, 55 (bottom); Walt Disney/
Photofest, 57; Muhammad Rehan/iStockphoto, 59; AP Images, 61; Win McNamee/
Getty Images, 63; Joshua Hodge Photography/iStockphoto, 67; Donald Traill/AP
Images, 68; Gregg DeGuire/PictureGroup via AP Images, 70; LM Otero/AP Images,
73; Nickolay Khoroshkov/Shutterstock, 75

Design Elements: Becky Daum/Red Line Editorial

Library of Congress Cataloging-in-Publication Data
Palser, Barb.
 Selling ourselves : marketing body images / by Barb Palser.
  p. cm.—(Media literacy)
Includes bibliographical references and index.
ISBN 978-0-7565-4519-2 (library binding)
ISBN 978-0-7565-4534-5 (paperback)
 1. Body image in children—Juvenile literature. 2. Body image in
adolescence—Juvenile literature 3. Self-acceptance—Juvenile literature.
I. Title.
BF723.B6P35 2012
306.4'613—dc23   2011025699

Visit Compass Point Books on the Internet at *www.capstonepub.com*

Printed in the United States of America in Stevens Point, Wisconsin.
102012   006968R

CONTENTS

CHAPTER 1

HOW DO YOU SEE YOURSELF?

> *"Everything has its beauty, but not everyone sees it."*
>
> —Chinese philosopher Confucius

What do you think about the way you look? Are you happy with your height, weight, hair, and eye color? Do you like your skin, nose, mouth, and ears? Is there anything you would change? How often do you think about how you look?

The way you think and feel about your body is called your body image. Your body image is part of your overall self-image—the way you feel about yourself as a whole person. That includes your personality, intelligence, and talents. For some people, body image is a big part of their self-image. For others, it's a very small part. A person with a positive body image is generally happy with his or her appearance. Someone with a negative body image is unhappy with his or her

appearance. These people often feel embarrassed to be seen by others.

Your body image is your opinion about yourself. It can be different from the way other people see you. People who are considered beautiful by society can have a negative body image. There are models and bodybuilders who think of themselves as ugly or flawed. On the other hand, many people who don't fit society's definition of beauty have a positive body image.

If your body image is an opinion in your mind, how does that opinion form? At what age does it begin to form? How do the media, entertainment, and advertising industries sway how you perceive yourself? Can your body image affect your life and health? By exploring these questions, you can become aware of how TV shows, movies,

A Calvin Klein billboard shows a dangerously skinny model. People may compare their own appearance to the models in advertisements. They may want to look like them. Or they may not.

magazines, and advertisements influence your ideas about beauty.

Developing a Body Image

Most people first experience the world through their families. Children watch their parents and siblings closely. They learn habits and opinions from those early role models. If a child's parent has a negative body image, the child may learn to have the same negative feelings about his or her own body.

Most people first experience the world through their families.

Children also absorb direct messages from other people. Children who are criticized for being stupid or overweight can believe those criticisms are true. Meanwhile, children who are praised for being smart and beautiful are more likely to see themselves that way.

As we grow up, our friends and peer groups affect us more. People often look at the height, weight, and general attractiveness of their peers to see how they measure up. This is especially true of teenagers, whose bodies mature at various speeds. The way a young person is treated by his or her peers can have a huge effect on that person's self-image and body image.

Whether body image is learned from others, molded by praise or criticism, or the result of comparison with others, a beauty standard is involved. This is an image, usually shared by a

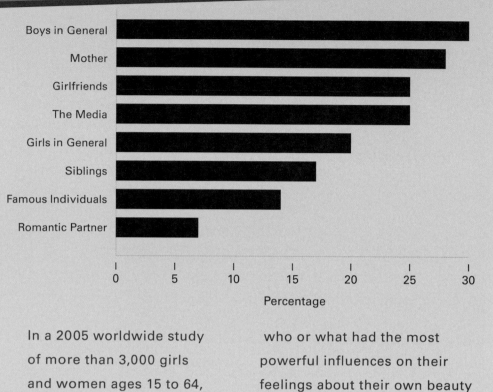

Percentage

In a 2005 worldwide study of more than 3,000 girls and women ages 15 to 64, researchers asked 100 American girls ages 15 to 17 who or what had the most powerful influences on their feelings about their own beauty and body image.

Source: "Beyond Stereotypes: Rebuilding the Foundation of Beauty Beliefs"

culture or social group, of what an ideal woman or man looks like. People tend to judge themselves and others based on a beauty standard.

Changing Beauty Standards

Various places in the world have differing beauty standards. Those standards change over time. For much of Western European history, heavy women were considered beautiful. Some of the most famous European paintings from the 1600s to the 1800s show women who are very plump and curvy. These women would be considered overweight by today's Western standards. Historians believe that round bodies were desirable because extra body fat was evidence of wealth. At a time when the average person struggled to get enough food to eat, only wealthy men and women could afford to gain extra weight. Meanwhile, muscular bodies and tan skin were not considered beautiful. They were signs of a lower-class life of manual labor.

Standards shifted in the 1900s. Fashion evolved and lifestyles changed. Western societies began to view excess weight as a sign of poor self-control and lack of discipline. Thinness became a sign of success and happiness. People—especially women—started to diet and exercise to lose weight.

Beauty standards are used not only to judge a person's appearance, but to judge his or her personality as well. In situations where food is plentiful, heavy people might be seen as lazy and undisciplined. In

UNUSUAL BEAUTY STANDARDS

Cultures have various ideas about beauty. The Maori people of New Zealand practice a type of face tattooing called Moko. It has been part of their culture for hundreds of years. The tattoos may be shocking to outsiders. However, they are beautiful and meaningful to the Maori people.

Women of the Kayan tribes in Thailand gradually stack brass coils around their necks to push down their collarbones and rib cages. This creates the appearance of very long necks. Tourists sometimes call these women "giraffe women."

the United States, people tend to connect negative personality traits with overweight people.

There are still places in the world today where heavy women are considered more attractive than thin women. In some West African countries, young girls are fattened in a custom called *leblouh*. The girls, as young as 5 years old, are forced to eat large quantities of food in order to make them attractive to potential husbands.

Until recently in Brazil, beautiful women were described as having a "guitar shape." That meant they had heavier lower bodies, including waist, hips, and thighs. But with the spread of Western media around the world, many Brazilian women are now using diet pills and having cosmetic surgery. They are attempting to get slim bodies like the American and European models and actresses they see.

"Giraffe women" in Thailand put coils around their necks to make their necks longer.········

Weight is not the only aspect of beauty standards. Americans spend billions of dollars each year on tanning products to make their skin darker. Meanwhile, Asians spend billions each year on bleaching products to lighten their skin. In each case, these people are trying to achieve a beauty standard.

Beauty Standards in the United States

For many years the ideals of American beauty for women and men resembled Barbie and Ken dolls—tall, thin, young, white, and often blond. Most of the models and actors who starred in glamorous movie roles and appeared in advertisements looked this way. In some ways that seems to be changing.

In a 1991 survey conducted by *Allure* magazine, blond-haired and blue-eyed model Christie Brinkley was chosen as the celebrity who best represented the ideal woman. When the survey was conducted again in 2011, the more exotic brunette Angelina Jolie was chosen as the most beautiful female celebrity.

Americans spend billions of dollars each year on tanning products to make their skin darker.

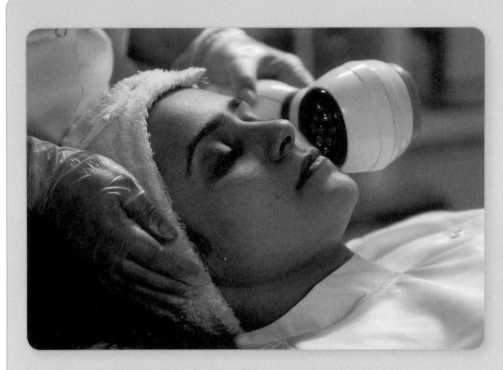

Some people with darker skin try to make it look lighter to achieve a beauty standard. Many attempt this by undergoing a cosmetic skin lightening procedure involving machines or special creams.

In the 2011 survey, 64 percent of people surveyed said that mixed-race women are the most beautiful women. Of the eight female celebrities chosen by men and women as the most beautiful, four were African-American or Hispanic. They were Halle Berry, Beyoncé Knowles, Jennifer Lopez, and Jessica Alba. Out of the 2,000 people surveyed, 70 percent wanted to have darker skin.

While beauty standards in the United States are changing to include various races and skin colors, there are still strong biases toward youth, thinness, and tallness. In the 2011 *Allure* survey, 93 percent of women said the pressure to look younger is greater than it's ever been. Ninety-seven percent of women and 86 percent of men said they wanted to lose weight. There are also biases toward smooth, clear skin and straight, shiny hair. People who weren't born with these features often go to great lengths to get them.

> *While beauty standards in the United States are changing to include various races and skin colors, there are still strong biases toward youth, thinness, and tallness.*

The United States has specific beauty standards for men as well. However, men generally feel less pressure than women to meet these ideals. American society promotes the idea that a muscular man is more masculine than a man without as much visible muscle or a man who is overweight. Male models for clothing brands such as Calvin Klein and Abercrombie & Fitch are often shown without shirts, displaying their muscular chests. In a 2000 study, the majority of men surveyed thought the ideal male body was 28 pounds (12.7 kilograms) more muscular than their own bodies. The majority

Advertisements use muscular male models to sell products to men because a muscular physique is seen as the ideal body type. · · · · · · · · · · · · · · · · ·

also thought that women preferred a more muscular man. However, when women were surveyed, most preferred a male body without a lot of muscle.

The Media's Role in Beauty Standards

Beauty standards would exist without the media. It's natural for societies to develop such standards. It makes sense that people want to be considered beautiful. Without the media we'd still compare ourselves to those around us.

However, modern media play a powerful role in supporting beauty standards. They also pressure people to live up to them. Some might even argue that today's media influence the way our beauty standards are defined.

One way the media support beauty standards is by providing role models—people who set examples for others to copy. There are many kinds of role models. They can be positive or negative. A classmate who finishes his homework on time and behaves well in class is a positive role model. So is a person who's honest and kind to others. Someone who lies or treats others badly is a negative role model. When it comes to body image, a role model is someone who looks or dresses a certain way. A positive body image role model is someone who sets an example of self-acceptance.

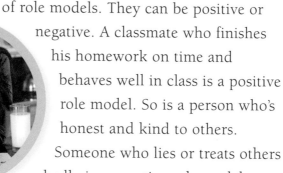

He or she encourages others to feel good about their appearance. A negative body image role model is someone who sets an example of unhealthy behavior or attitudes about appearance.

> *A positive body image role model is someone who sets an example of self-acceptance.*

A dangerously thin runway model is a negative body image role model for young girls. An actress with a healthy weight could be a positive role model. A negative role model for young men could be a bodybuilder who uses steroids. A positive role model could be a famous athlete who stays in shape without the use of drugs or extreme exercise and dieting. People often become confused about which role models they should follow.

Implied Media Messages

The media's use of role models is usually implied and unconscious. For example, companies that make beauty products choose attractive people to act in their commercials. A commercial for men's deodorant would probably show men who are handsome and in great physical shape. The company isn't promising that if men buy their deodorant they'll magically become handsome and fit. Still, the implied message is that handsome men use that brand of deodorant. Logical people would not expect a deodorant to make them more attractive. However, they may subconsciously wish to be like the role models they see in the commercials. They may subconsciously think that product can make them feel better about themselves. In the advertising industry, it's commonly known that "beauty sells."

Ads, TV shows, and movies starring thin people with clear skin and smooth hair are one way the media support society's beauty standard. They send the implied message that physical beauty is important to being successful, happy, and loved.

Explicit Media Messages

Not all media messages about beauty are implicit. Some, usually advertisements, are explicit.

> **Not all media messages about beauty are implicit.**

In a commercial for Jenny Craig weight loss products, actress Sara Rue talked about her 50-pound (22.7 kg) weight loss. She said, "When you feel good—really good—you can go anywhere, do anything ... This is me, 50 pounds gone.

Actress and Jenny Craig spokesperson Sara Rue promotes the idea that being thin and beautiful makes you happy. However, not all thin, beautiful people are happy with themselves or the way they look. . . . .

Now I can do anything. And for me, that's worth everything. You can do it too."

This is common language for weight loss ads. It sends the explicit message that thinness leads to freedom and happiness. Jenny Craig's slogan is "We Change Lives." For many people losing weight and getting fit can certainly lead to improved self-confidence and a more active social life. Research has even shown that aerobic exercise can

THE "OLD SPICE MAN"

Starting in 2010 Procter & Gamble, the makers of men's Old Spice bodywash, aired a series of unique TV commercials. The commercials made fun of the advertising industry's use of ideal physical role models. In the ads the handsome "Old Spice Man" is shown in various exaggerated scenes meant to represent women's romantic fantasies. He presents slogans such as "The man your man could smell like" and "Anything is possible when your man smells like Old Spice." The ads were a huge hit with the public, with tens of millions of views on the Internet. By encouraging people to laugh at the silliness of glamorizing a product like bodywash, Old Spice gained a lot of new fans. Sales of the product went up.

improve a person's mood for several hours afterward.

However, there is widespread agreement among psychologists and researchers that happiness and weight loss don't go hand-in-hand. They say the happiest people are those who spend a lot of time with friends and family, don't compare themselves to others, and practice gratitude and forgiveness. Thinness does not automatically lead to happiness. A thin person can be just as depressed or lonely as anyone else.

For many people losing weight and getting fit can certainly lead to improved self-confidence and a more active social life.

Can you think of any examples of implicit or explicit media messages about beauty? Have you ever wished you could look like a person in an advertisement, TV show, or movie? Do advertisements ever make you believe you'd be happier if you had different clothes, hair, or a different body shape?

CHAPTER 2

LIKING WHAT YOU SEE

> *"They [models] make me sick. They are too thin. But I would kill for one of their bodies."*
>
> —*Beth, a 25-year-old female participant in a research study on body image*

Most people don't fit society's beauty standard. Real people come in all shapes and sizes. Their bodies may be tall or short, heavy or slim. They might have big noses, crooked teeth, or ears that stick out. Very few people have flawless hair or skin.

Many people—especially those who already feel insecure about their bodies—compare themselves to others around them and to media role models. Sometimes comparing oneself to physical role models can have a positive effect. Seeing a celebrity or a contestant lose a lot of weight on a TV show can motivate some people. They might be inspired to achieve their goals just like

the role model. This is especially true if the role model is someone with whom they can relate.

More often, comparing oneself to role models in one's life or in the media has a negative effect. The consequences can be as minor as feeling badly for a few minutes. Or they can be as severe as a life-threatening health problem.

Low Self-Esteem and Depression

People with negative body images generally want to hide the parts of their bodies they're ashamed of. In severe cases this urge to hide can stand in the way of social relationships. It can lead the person to become isolated and even more ashamed and depressed. Sometimes people can become so obsessed about one aspect of their body that they aren't able to enjoy life.

WHAT'S AVERAGE?

The average American man is approximately 5 feet 9 inches (175 centimeters) tall and weighs approximately 195 pounds (88.5 kg). Male models are around 6 feet (183 cm) tall and can weigh between 140 and 160 pounds (63.5 and 72.6 kg), depending on how muscular they are.

The average American woman is approximately 5 feet 4 inches (163 cm) tall and weighs 165 pounds (74.8 kg). Female runway models are usually six inches taller at 5 feet 10 inches (178 cm) or 5 feet 11 inches (180 cm) and weigh less than 125 pounds (56.7 kg). For example, Victoria's Secret model Miranda Kerr is reportedly 5 feet 9 inches (175 cm) and 108 pounds (49 kg).

A survey found that 71 percent of American girls and women ages 15 to 64 said they had avoided certain activities because they felt badly about their looks. The most commonly avoided activities were going to the beach or pool, shopping for clothes, going to a social event, doing physical activities or sports, and trying out for a team or club.

It's possible that people who feel overweight might be encouraged by thin and fit role models to start exercising. But experts say it's more common for them to avoid exercising because they don't want anyone to see their bodies. By not exercising, they might gain even more weight and feel even worse.

Eating Disorders

Eating disorders are a group of health conditions in which people develop eating behaviors that threaten their mental and physical health. The disorders can even cause death. There are three main types of eating disorders.

People with anorexia nervosa have a distorted body image. They see themselves as overweight even when they are dangerously thin. They reduce their food consumption so much that their bodies start to break down. Sometimes they even starve themselves to death.

People with bulimia nervosa eat massive amounts of food at one time. Then they get rid of it by forcing themselves to throw up or by taking drugs that cause diarrhea. Uncontrolled eating is known as bingeing. The forced elimination of food is known as purging.

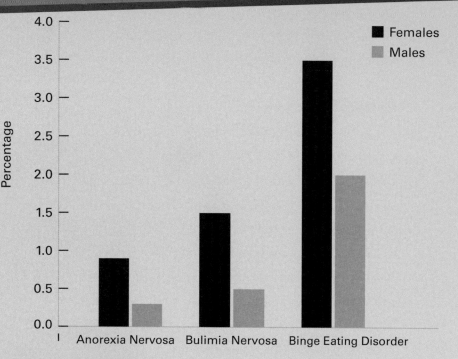

An estimated 24 million Americans will suffer from an eating disorder at some point in their lives. While girls and women are more likely to have eating disorders, the rate among boys and men is higher than previously thought.

Source: National Institute of Mental Health and McLean Hospital

A person with a binge eating disorder has episodes of uncontrolled eating but does not purge the food afterward.

It is also common for people with eating disorders to exercise obsessively. They do this to rid their bodies of the calories they have consumed. It's also common for those with eating disorders to suffer from depression.

A person with a binge eating disorder has episodes of uncontrolled eating but does not purge the food afterward.

Some possible causes of eating disorders, such as abuse or other trauma in a person's life, have nothing to do with body image or weight. But for athletes in certain sports, such as gymnastics or wrestling, the pressure to be a certain weight can lead to eating disorders. Low self-esteem and negative body image are common among people with eating disorders.

Complications from Cosmetic Procedures

Americans spent nearly $10.7 billion on cosmetic procedures in 2010, according to the American Society for Aesthetic Plastic Surgery. This includes surgical cosmetic procedures, such as breast enhancement or reduction, facelifts, nose reshaping, and liposuction to remove unwanted fat. It also includes nonsurgical cosmetic treatments, such as injections to fill in wrinkles, laser hair

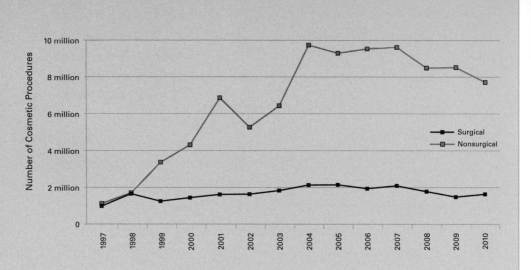

In 2010 more than 9 million surgical and nonsurgical cosmetic procedures were performed in the United States.

Source: The American Society for Aesthetic Plastic Surgery

removal, and treatments to reduce the appearance of veins. Ninety-two percent of all procedures were performed on women.

Some people get reconstructive plastic surgery. This is to correct birth defects or to rebuild body parts that have been damaged by accidents or diseases. In the United States millions more seek out expensive and painful procedures for the sake of improving their appearance. They believe that changing a body part (or multiple body parts) will improve not only their body image, but also their confidence and happiness.

Whether you believe cosmetic procedures are vain and selfish or simply a way for people to become happy with themselves, these procedures involve risks. With surgical and many nonsurgical procedures, patients can develop serious infections. They might become disfigured if the procedures don't go as planned.

As with other types of surgery, there's a small risk of death with cosmetic surgery. In 2007 the mother of rap star Kanye West died the day after she had plastic surgery. In 2009 Solange Magnano, a former Miss Argentina, died after surgery to enhance her buttocks.

The greatest risks are taken by people who go to underground "black market" practitioners for cheap and

As with other types of surgery, there's a small risk of death with cosmetic surgery.

Charmaine Rose holds up a cardboard cutout of herself made prior to her cosmetic procedures. As part of the reality show *Extreme Makeover UK*, Rose had a facelift, browlift, nose reconstruction, collagen injections in her lips, and several other cosmetic procedures.

illegal procedures. Every so often the media report stories of people who have been disfigured or even killed by illegal procedures conducted in private homes or unlicensed facilities.

Steroid Side Effects

While women account for most cosmetic surgeries, men are more likely to attempt to modify their bodies with anabolic steroids. While women tend to focus on their weight, men usually focus on their muscles. Some hope to develop the idealized V-shaped body with broad shoulders, muscular arms, and small waist. Anabolic steroids enhance muscle growth, but with some scary side effects. They include extreme mood swings, severe liver damage, high blood pressure, infertility, and stunted growth among adolescents.

While women account for most cosmetic surgeries, men are more likely to attempt to modify their bodies with anabolic steroids.

While many men and boys say they use steroids to improve their athletic abilities, researchers have found that physical appearance is also a significant reason. Sometimes it is the main reason. Some men develop muscle dysmorphia, in which they think their bodies are not muscular enough. They take steroids and exercise in a never-ending quest to build more muscle. The U.S. government estimates that 1.4 percent of both eighth- and 10th-grade

Former superstar Barry Bonds is a central figure in Major League Baseball's steroid scandal. A jury found him guilty of obstruction of justice in 2011.

students have used anabolic steroids, and 2.2 percent of 12th-grade students have used them. The majority of steroid users are male.

Skin Cancer

While people under 18 represent a small percentage of those who get cosmetic surgery, they make up a large percentage of people who risk developing skin cancer. Approximately 81 percent of white, non-Hispanic girls and women between the ages of 14 and 22 tan their bodies by exposing themselves to the sun. Approximately 32 percent use indoor tanning beds.

Studies show that indoor tanning increases a person's risk of developing melanoma, a type of skin cancer, by 75 percent. Most skin cancer deaths are caused by melanoma. "I have had patients—young women with a history using tanning beds—who have died from melanoma," said the president of the American Academy of Dermatology.

Why do you think some people take unhealthy measures in order to change their appearance? Why are some people obsessed with physical beauty, while others don't seem to worry about it at all? Why do you think that women and girls are more likely to suffer from eating disorders and to get plastic surgery than men and boys?

CHAPTER 3

IMPOSSIBLE STANDARDS

"In the end, you simply can't sell a beauty product without somehow playing on women's insecurities. If women thought they looked perfect—just the way they are—why would they buy anything?"

—Seth Stevenson, author of "When Tush Comes to Dove," Slate.com

For people whose ideas of beauty are defined by media images, there's a big problem. Many of the images we see in the media aren't real. In many cases it's impossible for a real human being to look like the images in magazines. Real-life models don't even look like their magazine photos.

For almost as long as photography has existed, there have been tricks for making people look better in pictures than in real life. By using special lights, makeup, and camera angles, photographers could make people look younger and slimmer than they actually were.

More recently computer software has allowed people to edit images with such exactness that most people would never guess that the image had been altered at all. It has become standard procedure for magazines and advertising agencies to use technology to make models and actors look flawless.

Image editing software can remove blotches and imperfections. The software replaces them with perfectly smooth, golden, glowing skin. It can remove unwanted pores, hairs, and freckles. It can whiten teeth and make lips appear glossy and full. It's often used to change the size and shape of body parts, creating thinner waists on women or bigger muscles on men. Most of the photos you see in magazines have been "improved" by graphic artists. News media are an exception. Most news magazines have rules against altering images.

Examples of Image Manipulation

Most of the time, altered photos are unnoticed or ignored. But when images of famous people are altered, it can be easier to notice because

> **Most of the time, altered photos are unnoticed or ignored.**

people have an idea of how a celebrity looks. Image manipulation has received some attention in the media.

- In July 2011 the United Kingdom banned cosmetics company L'Oréal's advertisements featuring actress Julia Roberts and supermodel Christy Turlington. The ads for antiaging foundation products, made by L'Oréal's Maybelline and Lancôme brands, were photoshopped and airbrushed to an extent that Britain's Advertising Standards Agency (ASA) considered the ads misleading. British politician Jo Swinson, who made the complaint to the  ASA, said, "Excessive airbrushing and digital manipulation techniques have become the norm, but both Christy Turlington and Julia Roberts are naturally beautiful women who don't need retouching to look great."

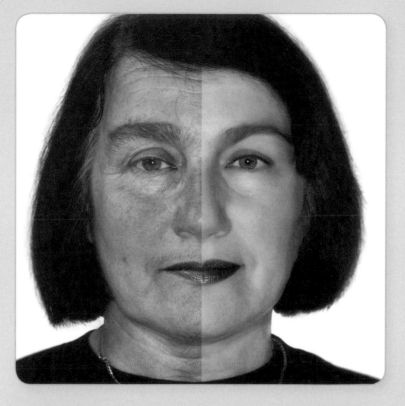

One half of this image has been altered. Images can be retouched to remove wrinkles and hair. Coloring and shapes can also be adjusted.

- In August 2010 the clothing store Ann Taylor displayed an altered image of a model on its website. The already-skinny model's body had been reduced dramatically at the hips, thighs, and waist. Ann Taylor apologized for the image. They said, "We want to support and celebrate the natural beauty of women, and we apologize if, in the process of retouching, that was lost."

- In its January 2010 issue, *OK!* magazine altered a photo of celebrity Kourtney Kardashian that was taken a week after she'd given birth. The altered image made it appear that she'd already lost all the weight from her pregnancy. The magazine then claimed to provide tips from Kardashian on how to quickly lose pregnancy weight. Kardashian explained that most of the magazine's facts were wrong. She said they "doctored and photoshopped my body to make it look like I have already lost all the weight, which I have not."

- In 2009 singer Kelly Clarkson appeared on the cover of *Self* magazine. She looked much slimmer than she had in other recent photos and TV appearances. The magazine's editor defended photo alteration. She said cover photos like Clarkson's "are not supposed to be a true-to-life snapshot," and are "meant to inspire women to want to be their best." Later the magazine said, "Magazines don't hide the fact that they're always trying to sell issues—and to sell copies, you need to appeal to readers with the best writing and the best images possible. No one wants to see a giant picture of some star's cellulite on the cover of a monthly mag."

Many images in the media and advertising have been retouched, but some companies are criticized for overly editing an image so that it is not realistic.

- In 2009 clothing company Ralph Lauren produced an ad for jeans featuring a female model whose image had been so slimmed that her head appeared to be wider than her waist. The company later apologized, admitting that their photo retouching had resulted in "a very distorted image of a woman's body." The model claimed she had been fired by Ralph Lauren for being too heavy.

- *Men's Fitness* magazine published a cover photo of tennis star Andy Roddick with larger-than-life arm muscles in 2007. Roddick wrote on his website, "Pretty sure I'm not as fit as this *Men's Fitness* cover suggests ... I walked by the newsstand in the airport and did a double take."

- In 2006 CBS altered a photograph of Katie Couric, the incoming anchor of *CBS Evening News*, to make her appear slimmer. The altered photograph appeared in *Watch!*, a magazine provided to CBS employees and American Airlines passengers. When the media discovered the alteration, the president of CBS News said he was surprised and disappointed to learn about it. Couric said she preferred the original, unaltered photograph.

Companies don't always admit to altering images. This can lead to controversy over whether such accusations are true.

Companies don't always admit to altering images. This can lead to controversy over whether such accusations are true. In 2008 cosmetics company L'Oréal Paris produced an ad for its Feria hair color products. The ad eatured Beyoncé Knowles with light-looking skin. The ad appeared in *Elle*, *Allure,* and *Essence* magazines. *Essence* magazine is targeted primarily to African-American women. People started comparing Beyoncé's skin color in the ad with other recent photographs that showed a darker tone. Despite the noticeable difference between the ad and Beyoncé's real-life appearance, L'Oréal Paris insisted they had not lightened her skin.

Dove Campaign for Real Beauty

In 2004 Unilever, the maker of Dove personal care products, launched an advertising strategy called the Dove Campaign for Real Beauty. The ad campaign featured so-called real women in magazines and on billboards. The women in the ads proudly showed off their curvy bodies, freckles, and natural-looking faces. The campaign later included messages encouraging positive body image and self-acceptance among older women and young girls.

As part of the campaign, Dove made a pledge to use real women—not models—in their advertisements. They also promised not to edit photographs to change the women's appearances. The company sponsored two worldwide studies

Most women don't look like the women seen on TV and in magazine ads. . . . .

about body image and self-esteem among women and girls. Through its Self-Esteem Fund, Dove hosts workshops for girls and their mentors.

While Dove has received a lot of praise for promoting realistic images of beauty, not everybody believes the company's efforts are completely sincere. Critics have pointed out that the original Campaign for Real Beauty ads were created to sell Dove's skin-firming products. In other words, the ads appeared to send the message that all women are beautiful just the way they are—but that they should buy Dove's skin-firming cream.

A 2008 article in *The New Yorker* magazine suggested that Campaign for Real Beauty photos had been altered by a professional digital artist. Dove strongly denied that claim. The company published a statement in which the photographer and digital artist were quoted. They said the only changes were minor color corrections and the removal of dust from the film.

What do you think? Do most people realize that the photos they see in magazines have probably been altered? Do you agree with the magazine editor who said such images should inspire women to be their best? Or are women being set up for disappointment by an impossible beauty standard?

CHAPTER 4

MIXED MESSAGES

> "People would come to me literally sobbing because they couldn't lose as much weight as we did in a week. But it's not real, it's TV."
>
> —The Biggest Loser *contestant Kai Hibbard*

If you were to buy a women's fashion magazine, you might find headlines like "Total Body Confidence" or "5 Reasons Your Body Is Perfect." On the same magazine cover, you might see headlines like "Be Hot by Saturday" or "Get Flat Abs Faster!" Inside the magazine you'd see ads for makeup, hair color, and diet products. Very few of the models in the ads would look like real women.

Every day we're bombarded with two kinds of messages. One message says, "You're fine just the way you are." The other says, "You'd be happier if you looked better." Which is the real message?

Some people might blame the media for sending mixed messages. Others would argue that the media are only showing the images people want to see. Beautiful, thin models are used to advertise products because beauty sells. The media and marketing industries are responding to the public's demand for miracle skin creams, magical hair products, and countless ways to lose weight.

The Biggest Loser

The popular TV show *The Biggest Loser* shows the public's obsession with miracle transformation. The show is an example of the positive and negative consequences of media messages that encourage aggressive steps for major weight loss. Contestants on the show are put through a strict program involving a low-calorie diet and several hours of exercise a day. They are supervised by professional dietitians and

Many magazines feature stories about how to get in shape or be beautiful.

trainers. At the end the contestant who has lost the greatest percentage of his or her starting body weight wins $250,000. With as many as 10 million viewers each week, *The Biggest Loser* has been credited with inspiring millions of overweight Americans to make positive changes in their lives. For viewers at home, seeing an average person lose massive amounts of weight can make the goal seem possible.

But the rapid weight loss portrayed on *The Biggest Loser* is not at all normal. There have been reports that contestants were allowed or even encouraged to engage in unhealthy behaviors in order to lose weight quickly. Former contestants have reported that dehydration is a common practice to achieve quick weight loss on the show. They've also said that when the TV cameras were off, contestants would exercise while wearing layers of heavy clothing. In 2009 a contestant had to be airlifted to a hospital after collapsing from heat stroke during a one-mile (1.6-kilometer) race. After that the doctors on the show made some changes. They started monitoring contestants' body temperatures when they were exercising.

While contestants on *The Biggest Loser* are sometimes portrayed as losing 15 pounds (6.8 kg) in a week, most doctors agree that losing more than one or two pounds (0.45 to 0.9 kg) per week is unsafe. Rapid weight loss can lead to

For viewers at home, seeing an average person lose massive amounts of weight can make the goal seem possible.

Opera singer Olivia Ward lost 129 pounds (58.5 kg)—nearly half her body weight—to become *The Biggest Loser* winner in 2011.

health problems such as dehydration, malnutrition, muscle loss, and chemical imbalances. Weight loss drugs can cause additional problems such as high blood pressure and increased heart rate.

Furthermore, research studies have shown that most people who diet to lose weight will gain all of the weight back, and sometimes more, within a few years. That is true of some TV show contestants. The winner of *The Biggest Loser*'s first season, Ryan C. Benson, lost 122 pounds (55.3 kg) on

EFFECTS OF MEDIA IMAGES ON WOMEN

Research has shown that when overweight women look at photographs of models, their self-esteem declines. Other research has shown that viewing magazine photos of women with thin, idealized bodies can improve body image for some women, but only for a short time. The coauthor of one such study explained it in the following way:

> *The media are saturated with images of idealized body shapes, which may make viewers and readers aspire to achieve the same. But it is a losing battle. Women are motivated by these fitness and beauty magazines to try to attain these supposedly perfect bodies, and may even get a short-term body image boost when they start dieting. However, research shows that most diets fail and they're eventually going to be back being unsatisfied with their bodies.*

the show. Four years later he was back to weighing more than 300 pounds (136 kg).

Internal Mixed Messages?

Perhaps the mixed messages we observe in the media reflect our own internal confusion about beauty and body image. Some people have competing voices in their own heads. On one hand, most people want to be healthy. On the other hand, they may be secretly craving an unhealthy level of thinness.

Perhaps the mixed messages we observe in the media reflect our own internal confusion about beauty and body image.

In surveys women often say that they know the skinny models in magazines are not realistic body image role models. These surveyed women say they'd like to see more "real women" in entertainment shows and magazines. Yet the same women may also say they are unhappy with their bodies and would give anything to look like those skinny models.

For example, in a 2004 survey of American women and girls, 87 percent said that beauty can be achieved through attitude, spirit, and other nonphysical qualities. However, in a 2005 follow-up survey, 92 percent of American women and girls

Some models are so skinny that you can see their bones. ....

wanted to change some aspect of their physical appearance. Body weight was the most commonly desired area of change (50 percent), followed by body shape (25 percent).

Almost all magazines admit to altering images to make them more idealistic. This can set an impossible standard of beauty for the magazine's readers.

What do you think? Are the media and advertising industries responsible for creating unrealistic expectations about weight loss and other beauty goals? Are companies setting people up to

In 2005 actress Jane Fonda, who was 67 at the time, refused to allow her cover photo for *Good Housekeeping* magazine to be altered to remove her wrinkles. "I don't want my wrinkles taken away—I want to look like everyone else," Fonda told the magazine. She made a second appearance on *Good Housekeeping*'s cover in 2011 at age 73, again refusing to allow her wrinkles to be erased. Yet Fonda had cosmetic surgery on her chin, neck, and eyes in 2010. "I wish I'd been brave enough not to do anything," Fonda wrote on her blog, "but instead, I chose to be a somewhat more glamorous grandma."

Fonda's mixed feelings about beauty and aging are common, especially among women. At times they may feel proud of their age and wish to set an example of self-acceptance. At other times the desire to look and feel young is very powerful.

feel badly about themselves so that they'll buy more products? Or are the media and advertisers just giving people what they want to see?

CHAPTER 5

CHILDREN AND TEENS

"She's the most beautiful girl in town. That makes her the best."

—Gaston, in Disney's **Beauty and the Beast**

At what age did you first start thinking about your appearance? When did you begin comparing your looks to the looks of others? Research has shown that children can start developing opinions about their bodies at a very early age. Some say that the U.S. culture of physical beauty and media messages directed toward children are causing children to form body images earlier than ever before.

Since it can be difficult to do accurate studies with young children, researchers have been uncertain about when children first develop opinions about their bodies. However, a 2009 study of 3- to 6-year-old girls found that half of them were concerned about being fat.

One out of three said they would like to change something about their appearance, such as their weight or their hair color.

Princes and Princesses

When you were a young child, you may have watched Disney movies such as *Cinderella*, *Beauty and the Beast,* or *The Little Mermaid.* Have you ever noticed that many fairy-tale movies involve beautiful maidens with tiny waists and long, flowing hair? Or that they are often saved by a handsome, muscular prince? (There are a few exceptions, such as the DreamWorks movie *Shrek*, in which the princess turns into an ogre instead of the other way around.)

What about the way the villains are portrayed? Think about the ugly stepsisters in *Cinderella* and the witch Ursula in *The Little Mermaid*. It's common in fairy tales throughout history for evil characters to be shown as ugly and often overweight.

Some parents worry that exposing their children, especially girls, to princess role models will lead to body image problems. In *Time* magazine one mother described how her 4-year-old girl cut off her curly hair because she'd noticed that Disney princesses all seemed to have straight hair. However, a research study in 2009 found that watching Disney movies did not seem to have a negative impact on girls' body images. After watching scenes from *Cinderella* and *Beauty and the Beast*, the girls in the study wanted to play-act as the princesses. But they did not seem to feel any worse about themselves than before watching the movies. In 2009 Disney released *The Princess and the Frog*, starring Tiana, Disney's first African-American, curly-haired animated princess. Tiana added diversity to Disney's collection of princess characters, but she

> **Some parents worry that exposing their children, especially girls, to princess role models will lead to body image problems.**

Tiana is Disney's first African-American princess. She is still very thin like the other Disney princesses.

was still very thin and shapely like those who came before her.

Beauty and Grooming Products

The media play a part in encouraging people to be concerned about their outward appearance from a young age. In fact, girls and teens today use makeup and hair-styling products at younger ages than ever before. In 2005 the average age for teen girls to start using beauty products was 17. By 2009 the average age was 13. Almost half of all 6- to 9-year-old girls use lipstick or lip gloss. Twelve percent use other makeup such as mascara. It's estimated that girls and teens spend around $1.6 billion a year on beauty products.

Advertisements for beauty products often connect the product to a beautiful celebrity or character. In 2010 Target stores started selling inexpensive Hello Kitty makeup. In 2011 Wal-Mart

PADDED BIKINI FOR GIRLS?

In 2011 the clothing store Abercrombie & Fitch started marketing a "push-up" bikini top for girls on its Abercrombie Kids website. The padded bikini top was available in sizes for girls as young as 7 or 8 years old. The company was immediately attacked by the media and angry parents. So they removed the phrase "push-up" from the product description. That change did not soothe the concerns of psychologists and parents. They remained outraged by the message that young girls should make their bodies look like an adult woman's.

launched the geoGirl brand of makeup, including lip gloss, eye shadow, and mascara.

For boys there has been an increase in the use of personal grooming products such as body spray, hair gel, and skin care products. Companies use celebrity role models, social media sites such as Facebook, video games, and funny YouTube commercials to reach boys and young men. An advertisement for Old Spice's Swagger scent featured

Body spray and hair-styling products are marketed to young teen boys.

rapper LL Cool J being transformed from a high school nerd to a macho man by using the product. When asked by a reporter why he used Axe body spray, one seventh-grade boy said, "I feel confident when I wear it." Some experts say it's concerning for companies to be encouraging preteens to focus on their appearance. Others say it's not necessarily harmful.

Childhood Obesity and Antifat Messages

The U.S. government estimates that around 17 percent of young Americans ages 2 to 19 are obese. Obesity is not just a few extra pounds. It's a condition in which a person's weight is so excessive that it impacts his or her health and quality of life. The risks of childhood obesity include high blood pressure, diabetes, breathing problems, asthma, liver disease, low self-esteem, and negative body image. Obese children often suffer bullying and teasing from their peers. This can cause them to withdraw from social interaction and feel even worse about themselves. "This kind of criticism tends to increase the victim's body dissatisfaction,"

The U.S. government estimates that around 17 percent of young Americans ages 2 to 19 are obese.

said one researcher. "It becomes something of a vicious cycle."

For an obese child or teen, seeing media images of the slender ideal body can add to his or her feelings of low self-worth. Media messages meant to discourage child obesity can be equally painful. In 2011 a children's health group in Georgia ran an advertising campaign against child obesity.

A Georgia campaign used photos of overweight children to raise awareness about childhood obesity. Many criticized the campaign for creating further stigma around kids already likely to be bullied.

OBESITY AMONG CHILDREN AND TEENS

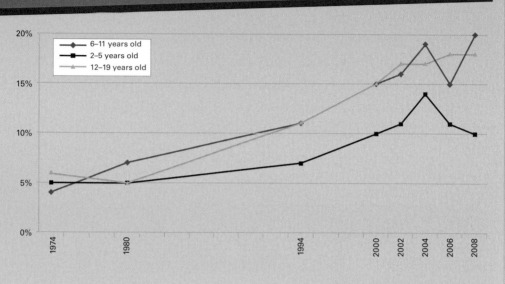

◆ 6–11 years old	
■ 2–5 years old	
▲ 12–19 years old	

Obesity among children and teens is on the rise. In 2008 19.6 percent of 6- to 11-year-olds and 18.1 percent of 12- to 19-year-olds were obese.

That's almost one out of every five people. Among 2- to 5-year-olds, the rate was 10.4 percent, or one in 10.

Source: Centers for Disease Control and Prevention

The campaign featured billboards and videos with pictures of overweight children and slogans such as "Chubby kids may not outlive their parents." The campaign was meant to get the attention of parents of overweight children.

Many parents and groups against weight discrimination were outraged. They said that the ads would result in more bullying of overweight children. One expert said that antifat messages tend to worsen the self-esteem of adults and children, making them more likely to eat unhealthy foods and avoid physical activity.

Interestingly, one of the overweight children whose photos were used for the ads went on TV to say that the campaign had improved her self-confidence. Before being asked to pose for the ads, the 14-year-old said, "I didn't feel pretty.

First lady Michelle Obama's Let's Move campaign battles childhood obesity by promoting exercise and healthy eating for kids and teens across the country. . . . .

I didn't feel like I could do anything like this because of my weight. Now I see somebody likes me just the way I am."

Risks for Children and Teens

The earlier in life people develop body image problems, the more serious and dangerous those problems can become. This is partly because young people are more likely to see a difficult situation as hopeless. They are also more likely to take risky measures without thinking them through.

It's estimated that 90 percent of people who suffer from eating disorders are females between 12 and 25 years old.

For example, harmful eating habits and disorders often start during the teenage and young adult years. It's estimated that 90 percent of people who suffer from eating disorders are females between 12 and 25 years old.

In the most extreme cases, stress and depression connected to negative self-image and bullying can lead to suicide. While the possibility of suicide may be increased by other factors in a teen's life, including drug abuse, mental illness, and traumatic life events, it has also been linked to self-esteem and body image. One study showed that teens who

Teens with negative self-images can develop eating disorders or depression that can even lead to suicide. ·

viewed themselves as very fat or very skinny were twice as likely as other teens to attempt or think about suicide.

What do you think? Is it OK for young girls to wear makeup or for young boys to use scented body sprays? What about antiobesity messages such as the Georgia campaign? Are such messages helpful in fighting childhood obesity, or do they do more harm than good?

CHAPTER 6

BORN BEAUTIFUL

"I'm beautiful in my way. 'Cause God makes no mistakes. I'm on the right track baby. I was born this way."

—Lyrics to Lady Gaga's song "Born This Way"

Children, teens, and adults in the United States are exposed to a constant stream of unrealistic images and implied messages about beauty from the media, entertainment, and advertising industries. In surveys people say the pressure to look young and slim is greater than ever before.

However, the number of positive messages and role models also seems to be growing. If you look, you can find individuals and groups who are challenging traditional beauty standards. While they might not be successful in changing the U.S. obsession with youth and body shape, they

could at least broaden our definition of beauty. Here are some examples:

- In 2010 an episode of *Sesame Street* featured an African-American puppet with natural hair singing a song called "I Love My Hair." The song became a hit on YouTube with millions of views. Mothers of African-American girls left comments on the Internet thanking *Sesame Street* for providing a positive body image role model for their children. The writer who created the song was inspired by his adopted daughter from Ethiopia. She had told him that she "wanted her hair to be long or blond like Barbie or a princess."
- The hit TV show *Glee* has been praised for showing high school characters of various ethnicities and sizes in positive roles. Several

The cast of *Glee* offers diversity in race and body type. But the main characters are played by thin actors. · · · · · · · · · · · · ·

episodes have focused on messages of self-acceptance and positive body image. In season two of the show, the handsome "bad boy" character, Puck, develops a crush on overweight Lauren. But critics have pointed out that the lead roles are still played by attractive, thin actors.

- Reality TV stars Kourtney, Kim, and Khloe Kardashian are celebrated for their beauty, including their figures. The Kardashians are curvier than the average model or Hollywood starlet. An untouched magazine photograph of Kim Kardashian was accidentally made public, showing her thighs in their natural state. Kim responded on her blog: "So what: I have a little cellulite. What curvy girl doesn't? I'm proud of my body and my curves … Just because I am on the cover of a magazine doesn't mean I'm perfect."

The Kardashians are curvier than the average model or Hollywood starlet.

- In 2008 Whitney Thompson became the first plus-sized model to win the reality TV competition *America's Next Top Model*. At size 10, Thompson was much closer to the size of an average woman than the typical size 2 model. "I personally would welcome more flesh on models," said one fashion industry executive. "I think that the … thin models on runways right now are unattractive, not alluring; they're starting to look old. It's starting to become tired. It makes sense that there should be a shift toward a fuller figure. They couldn't get any thinner than they are now."

In 2008 Whitney Thompson became the first plus-sized model to win *America's Next Top Model*. At a size 10, she is still slimmer than many American women. ·

• Some TV and movie studios are starting to turn down actresses who've had plastic surgery in favor of women with a more natural appearance. When the Walt Disney Company was looking for people to act as extras in a *Pirates of the Caribbean* movie in 2010, they specifically screened out women who'd had breast enhancement surgery. Hollywood executives say one reason for this trend is that many women end up looking fake after cosmetic procedures. "It is viewed as ridiculous," one movie director and producer said. "Ten years ago, actresses felt that they had to get plastic surgery to get the part. Now I think it works against them. To walk into a casting session looking false hurts one's chances."

What You Can Do

Since advertising and media are everywhere you look, it would be almost impossible to avoid messages about what beauty is and which products

BARBIE AND KEN

In 1996 researchers at the University of South Australia determined that the odds of a real woman having the body shape of a Barbie doll are less than one in 100,000. They found that the chances of a man having the body shape of a Ken doll are around one in 50. Over the years Barbie in particular has been criticized for portraying unrealistic and unhealthy ideas about female identity and beauty.

you should buy to achieve it. Here are some things to remember about those messages:

- The goal of an advertisement is to make you feel unsatisfied or incomplete. This is achieved by suggesting that the advertised product has the power to make you happy, popular, or successful. It's harder to sell a diet or beauty product to someone who's content with the way he or she is.
- Look for mixed messages in TV shows, movies, and other media. A show or a movie might be sending an explicit message of self-acceptance, but do the actors and actresses look like normal people? Or are they unrealistically slim and attractive?

It's harder to sell a diet or beauty product to someone who's content with the way he or she is.

- Seek out positive messages and body image role models. Instead of wishing to change yourself, look for TV shows, movies, music artists, websites, books, and activities that make you feel good about yourself.
- If you feel self-conscious about your appearance, talk to an adult family member or friend. Your friends and loved ones might help you see yourself in a more positive light. You might

Girls in Motion of Dallas, Texas, and similar programs are aimed at creating positive body image and promoting healthy living. ·

discover that almost everyone is self-conscious about something.

Finally, remember that achieving society's beauty standard is impossible for most people. The few who achieve it aren't necessarily any happier than the rest of us. In fact, people who spend their lives pursuing physical beauty are less likely to feel fulfilled. Instead of allowing media messages to tell you how to be happy, think about your own unique skills, interests, and relationships. Decide what happiness means to you.

MEDIA LITERACY 101

Here are some exercises that will help you think critically about body image and beauty messages in the media:

1 Think of a person in your real life whom you admire. The person could be a parent or another adult, a sister or brother, a friend, or anyone else you know and respect. Then write a list of five reasons why you like this person.

Next, think about a person in the media who represents society's beauty standard. The person might be an actor or actress, a model, or an attractive athlete. Write a list of five things that describe that person.

Compare your two lists. Which list do you think describes a more likable person?

2 By clipping images from magazines, create a collage that represents the things that make you feel happy and good about yourself. You can use pictures of people, animals, landscapes, or objects. When you've finished your collage, ask yourself:

How many of the pictures you selected are about physical beauty?

How many of the pictures you selected are about objects or products you'd like to have?

How many of the pictures you selected are about activities you enjoy?

If a stranger looked at your collage, what assumptions might he or she make about you?

3 Watch an hour of TV. For every commercial you see, make a note of what the commercial is advertising. Also make a note of whether an attractive person is used to sell a product. For example, an attractive woman might appear in a commercial for breakfast cereal, or an attractive man might appear in a car commercial.

When you're done, count the total number of commercials you watched.

Then count the number of commercials that advertised products designed to make a person more physically attractive, such as makeup, hair color, body spray, diet products, or exercise equipment.

Finally, count the number of commercials that used an attractive man or woman, regardless of what was being advertised.

In one hour of television, how often was beauty—or the promise of beauty—used to sell something?

GLOSSARY

anabolic steroids
drugs that enhance muscle growth, often with dangerous side effects

anorexia nervosa
an eating disorder in which the sufferer sees himself or herself as overweight, even when he or she is thin, and reduces food consumption to dangerous levels

beauty standard
an image, usually shared by a culture or social group, of what an ideal man or woman looks like

binge eating disorder
an eating disorder in which the sufferer has episodes of uncontrolled eating

bulimia nervosa
an eating disorder in which the sufferer eats large quantities of food and then eliminates it through forced vomiting or diarrhea

dehydration
depriving the body of water

explicit message
information presented in an obvious way

implied message
information suggested or hinted at, without being outwardly stated

leblouh
a West African custom in which young girls are forced to overeat to make them heavier and more attractive to a future husband

muscle dysmorphia
a disorder in which the sufferer perceives his or her body as less muscular than it is, using excessive exercise and sometimes steroids in a never-ending quest to build more muscle

obesity
a condition in which a person is significantly overweight

Investigate Further

Hirschmann, Kris. *Reflections of Me: Girls and Body Image*. Mankato, Minn.: Compass Point Books, 2009.

Lankford, Ronald D. *Body Image*. Detroit: Lucent, 2010.

Rutledge, Jill Zimmerman. *Picture Perfect: What You Need to Feel Better About Your Body*. Deerfield Beach, Fla.: Health Communications, 2007.

Williams, Heidi. *Body Image*. Farmington Hills, Mich.: Greenhaven, 2009.

Woog, Adam. *Mirror Image: How Guys See Themselves*. Mankato, Minn.: Compass Point Books, 2009.

Internet Sites

Use FactHound to find Internet sites related to this book. All of the sites on FactHound have been researched by our staff.

Here's all you do:

Visit *www.facthound.com*

Type in this code: 9780756545192

Keep Exploring Media Literacy!

Read the other books in this series:

The Big Push: *How Popular Culture Is Always Selling*
Choosing News: *What Gets Reported and Why*
Violence as Entertainment: *Why Aggression Sells*

SOURCE NOTES

Chapter 1

Page 4, opening quote: Joey Green. *Philosophy on the Go.* Philadelphia: Running Press, 1994, p. 91.

Page 8, graph: Nancy Etcoff, et al. "Beyond Stereotypes: Rebuilding the Foundation of Beauty Beliefs—Findings of the 2005 Dove Global Study." 19 Oct. 2011. www. vawpreventionscotland.org.uk/sites/default/files/Dove%20 Beyond%20Stereotypes%20White%20Paper.pdf

Page 12, line 14: Deborah Dunham. "Mixed Race Is Epitome of American Beauty, *Allure* Survey Reveals." Stylelist.com. 9 March 2011. 30 Aug. 2011. www.stylelist. com/2011/03/09/mixed-race-american-beauty-allure-survey

Page 14, line 4: Alison Caporimo. "What's Beautiful Now: The *Allure* American Beauty Survey." Allure.com. 30 Aug. 2011. www.allure.com/beauty-trends/2011/american-beauty-census

Page 14, line 23: Nancy Clark. "Mirror, mirror on the wall … are muscular men the best of all? The hidden turmoil of muscle dysmorphia–Nutrition." *American Fitness.* February 2004. 30 Aug. 2011. findarticles.com/p/articles/ mi_m0675/is_1_22/ai_112408511

Page 18, line 20: "Sara Rue." Jenny Craig. 30 Aug. 2011. www.jennycraig.com/commercial/sara

Chapter 2

Page 22, opening quote: Sarah Grogan. *Body Image: Understanding Body Dissatisfaction in Men, Women, and Children.* New York: Routledge, 2008, p. 51.

Page 24, line 1: "Beyond Stereotypes: Rebuilding the Foundation of Beauty Beliefs—Findings of the 2005 Dove Global Study."

Page 26, graph: "First National Survey on Eating Disorders Finds Binge Eating More Common Than Other Eating Disorders." McLean Hospital. 1 Feb. 2007. 30 Aug. 2011. www.mclean.harvard.edu/news/press/current.php?id=103

Page 28, graph: "Statistics." American Society for Aesthetic Plastic Surgery. 3 Oct. 2011. www.surgery.org/media/statistics

Page 31, line 24: "NIDA InfoFacts: Steroids." National Institute on Drug Abuse. July 2009. 30 Aug. 2011. www. nida.nih.gov/infofacts/steroids.html

Page 33, line 9: "New survey finds teen girls and young women need a lesson on dangers of indoor tanning." American Academy of Dermatology. 2 May 2011. 30 Aug. 2011. www.aad.org/stories-and-news/news-releases/new-survey-finds-teen-girls-and-young-women-need-a-lesson-on-dangers-of-indoor-tanning-

Chapter 3

Page 34, opening quote: Seth Stevenson. "When Tush Comes to Dove." Slate.com. 1 Aug. 2005. 7 July 2011. www.slate.com/id/2123659

Page 36, line 18: Bryony Jones. "Britain Bans Airbrushed Julia Roberts Make-up Ad." CNN. com. 28 July 2011. 5 Aug. 2011. http://edition. cnn.com/2011/WORLD/europe/07/28/airbrushed. advertisements.ban/index.html

Page 37, line 6: "Photoshopping: Altering Images and Our Minds!" BeautyRedefined. 24 Feb. 2011. 7 July 2011. www.beautyredefined.net/ photoshopping-altering-images-and-our-minds

Page 38, line 9: "*OK!* Helps Kourtney Shed Baby Weight With Photoshop Phony Diet." Jezebel. 25 Jan. 2010. 7 July 2011. http://jezebel.com/5456336/ ok-helps-kourtney-shed-baby-weight-with-photoshop-phony-diet

Page 38, line 18: Lucy Danziger. "Lucy's Blog: Pictures that please us." Self.com. 10 Aug. 2009. 30 Aug. 2011. www.self.com/magazine/blogs/ lucysblog/2009/08/pictures-that-please-us.html

Page 38, line 21: Ashley Mateo. "SELFy Stars: The wonders of PhotoShop." Self.com. 10 Aug. 2009. 30 Aug. 2011. www.self.com/magazine/blogs/ selfystars/2009/08/the-wonders-of-photoshop.html

Page 39, line 6: "Ralph Lauren apologises for digitally retouching slender model to make her head look bigger than her waist." *Mail* Online. 10 Oct. 2009. 19 Oct. 2011. www.dailymail.co.uk/news/ worldnews/article-1219046/Ralph-Lauren-digitally-retouches-slender-model-make-look-THINNER.html

Page 40, line 4: "Andy Roddick Is Not That Jacked Up." Deadspin. 22 May 2007. 30 Aug. 2011. http:// deadspin.com/#!262537/andy-roddick-is-not-that-jacked-up

Chapter 4

Page 44, opening quote: Eric Deggans. "Former 'Biggest Loser' competitor Kai Hibbard calls the show unhealthy, misleading." *St. Petersburg Times.*. 4 April 2010. 7 July 2011. www.tampabay.com/features/ media/former-biggest-loser-competitor-kai-hibbard-calls-the-show-unhealthy/1084764

Page 49, sidebar, line 13: "Media's Focus on Ideal Body Shape Can Boost Women's Body Satisfaction —For a While." The Ohio State University. 11 April 2011. 30 Aug. 2011. http://researchnews.osu.edu/ archive/thinideal.htm

Page 50, line 20: "The Real Truth About Beauty: A Global Report Fact Sheet." 19 Oct. 2011. www.docstoc.com/docs/28381032/The-Real-Truth-About-Beauty-A-Global-Report-Fact-Sheet

Page 50, line 23: "Beyond Stereotypes: Rebuilding the Foundation of Beauty Beliefs — Findings of the 2005 Dove Global Study."

Page 53, sidebar, line 6: Caroline Davies. "Fonda at 67 refuses to hide her wrinkles." *The Telegraph.* 9 Sept. 2005. 30 Aug. 2011. www.telegraph.co.uk/news/worldnews/northamerica/usa/1498035/Fonda-at-67-refuses-to-hide-her-wrinkles.html

Page 53, sidebar, line 16: Jane Fonda. "Valentine's Day—A Little Late." JaneFonda.com. 16 Feb. 2010. 30 Aug. 2011. http://janefonda.com/valentine%E2%80%99s-day%E2%80%94a-little-late

Chapter 5

Page 54, opening quote: "'Too Fat to Be a Princess?' Young Girls Worry About Body Image, Study Shows." *Science Daily.* 24 Nov. 2009. 19 Oct. 2011. www.sciencedaily.com/releases/2009/11/091124103615.htm

Page 54, col. 2, line 9: Ibid.

Page 56, line 14: Ibid.

Page 58, line 1: Jessica Bennett. "Generation Diva." *Newsweek.* 29 March 2009. 30 Aug. 2011. www.newsweek.com/2009/03/29/generation-diva.html

Page 60, line 4: Jan Hoffman. "Masculinity in a Spray Can." *The New York Times.* 29 Jan. 2010. 30 Aug. 2011. www.nytimes.com/2010/01/31/fashion/31smell.html

Page 60, line 9: "Obesity rates among all children in the United States." CDC.gov. 19 Oct. 2011. www.cdc.gov/obesity/childhood/data.html

Page 60, line 22: Steve Smith. "Study: Teasing about weight can have big effects on pre-teens." University of Nebraska-Lincoln. 14 Sept. 2010. 30 Aug. 2011. http://newsroom.unl.edu/announce/todayatunl/61/593

Page 62, graph: Cynthia Ogden and Margaret Carroll. "Prevalence of Obesity Among Children and Adolescents: United States, Trends 1963-1965 Through 2007-2008." CDC.gov. 4 June 2010. 30 Aug. 2011. www.cdc.gov/nchs/data/hestat/obesity_child_07_08/obesity_child_07_08.htm

Page 63, line 12: Seamus McGraw. "Teen actress: Anti-obesity ads made me more confident."Today.com. 6 May 2011. 30 Aug. 2011. http://today.msnbc.msn.com/id/42929825/ns/today-today_health

Chapter 6

Page 66, opening quote: "Born This Way" lyrics. 19 Oct. 2011. www.ladygaga.com/news/default.aspx?nid=33476

Page 67, line 12: Melanie Sims. "Curly-haired Muppet is role model for black girls." *USAToday.* 20 Oct. 2010. 19 Oct. 2011. www.usatoday.com/life/television/news/2010-10-20-sesame-street-hair_N.htm

Page 69, line 6: Kim Kardashian. "Yes, I Am Complex!" Celebuzz. 25 March 2009. 30 Aug. 2011. http://kimkardashian.celebuzz.com/2009/03/25/yes_i_am_complex

Page 69, line 18: Sheila Marikar. "Skinny Models Out, Plus-Size In?" ABC News. 19 May 2008. 30 Aug. 2011. http://abcnews.go.com/Entertainment/story?id=4873965

Page 71, line 5: Laura M. Holson. "A Little Too Ready For Her Close-Up?" *The New York Times.* 23 April 2010. 19 Oct. 2011. www.nytimes.com/2010/04/25/fashion/25natural.html

Page 71, sidebar, line 1: Kevin I. Norton,et. al. "Ken and Barbie at Life Size." *Sex Roles, Vol. 34 (3–4).* February 1996, pp. 287–294. 19 Oct. 2011. http://psycnet.apa.org/?&fa=main.doiLanding&uid=1996-05312-008

SELECT BIBLIOGRAPHY

BeautyRedefined. www.beautyredefined.net

Etcoff, Nancy, et al. "Beyond Stereotypes: Rebuilding the Foundation of Beauty Beliefs—Findings of the 2005 Dove Global Study." www.vawpreventionscotland.org.uk/sites/default/files/Dove%20Beyond%20Stereotypes%20White%20Paper.pdf

Grogan, Sarah. *Body Image: Understanding Body Dissatisfaction in Men, Women, and Children.* New York: Routledge, 2008.

"The Real Truth About Beauty: A Global Report Fact Sheet." www.docstoc.com/docs/28381032/The-Real-Truth-About-Beauty-A-Global-Report-Fact-Sheet

INDEX

ABOUT THE AUTHOR

Barb Palser is director of digital media at McGraw-Hill Broadcasting Company, where she oversees four local TV station websites. She is also a regular columnist and feature writer for *American Journalism Review*, a magazine for journalists and journalism students.